UNIVERSITY BOOKSTORE

A CORPORATE PRACTICE SET FOR USE WITH ACCOUNTING PRINCIPLES

SALLY NELSON
Northeast Iowa Community College
Peosta, Iowa

CANDACE HUMPHREY
University of Dubuque
Dubuque, Iowa

JOHN WILEY & SONS, INC.
New York • Chichester • Weinheim • Brisbane • Singapore • Toronto

COVER PHOTO © James Bareham/Stone.

To order books or for customer service call 1-800-CALL-WILEY (225-5945).

ISBN 0-471-39155-7

Printed in the United States of America

10 9 8 7 6 5 4 3 2 1

Printed and bound by Victor Graphics, Inc.

Contents

INTRODUCTION

The objective of the University Bookstore, Inc., practice set is to expose you (the student) to a simulation of maintaining a set of books for a small retail corporation. In order to keep the number of entries to a minimum (therefore reducing the amount of pencil pushing), you will be recording transactions for only one week. You will find that this is a busy company during this one-week period.

You will also find that you have to think a bit (or even look up something in your text) on some of the transactions.

The authors recommend this practice set anytime after corporations and bonds payable/present value topics have been covered. The most likely place for its use is at the end of Financial Accounting, after bonds payable in the second semester of Accounting Principles, or at the beginning of Intermediate Accounting (to provide a review of accounting procedures).

INSTRUCTIONS

Complete the requirements listed below, following proper accounting procedures and format. The Chart of Accounts, May 24, 2002, Trial Balance, Present Value tables and necessary accounting papers are provided.

The May 24, 2002, Trial Balance and a calendar for the Month of May 2002 are given on pages 22, 23 and 24.

Requirements:

1. Ask your professor what version you will be using.

2. Journalize and post the transactions starting on the page titled Journal Entries for the version you are instructed to use **(round all transactions and computations in this practice set to the nearest dollar).**

3. Prepare a Trial Balance on the worksheet provided at the back of this book.

4. Complete the worksheet using the information shown on the page titled "End of Fiscal Year Information" for the version assigned by your instructor. In addition you will need the May 31, 2002, Trial Balance to complete the necessary adjusting entries.

5. Prepare a Multi-step Income Statement, a Statement of Retained Earnings, and a Classified Balance Sheet (all in good form). Your professor may also instruct you to prepare a Statement of Cash Flows.

6. Journalize and post the adjusting entries.

7. Journalize and post the closing entries.

8. Prepare a Post Closing Trial Balance.

9. Answer the Financial Analysis questions (starting on page 19) that your professor has assigned, plus any additional questions your professor may provide. Use the June 1, 2001, Balance Sheet for your beginning balances.

COMPANY INFORMATION
UNIVERSITY BOOKSTORE, INC.

University Bookstore, Inc. is located on the campus of Fictitious University in University City, Iowa. The bookstore sells new and used texts, selected other books, supplies, stationery products, software, soft goods (sweatshirts, sweatpants, etc.), and miscellaneous items to students and faculty. Also, the bookstore sells supplies to various university departments. University Bookstore, Inc., was incorporated in the state of Iowa on June 1, 1992, and operates on a fiscal year ending May 31. The bookstore is authorized to issue 5,000 shares of 8%, $100 par value cumulative, non-participating preferred stock and 500,000 shares of $5 par value common stock.

The bookstore employs a manager, a full-time clerk, part-time sales help (as needed), and a part-time accounting major to maintain the accounting records. Andrew Kelly (the part-time accounting major) submitted his resignation for this position effective May 24, 2002. He graduated in May, and has obtained a full-time accounting position. Mr. Kelly has recorded and posted transactions up to and including May 24. He has provided you with a printed trial balance dated May 24, 2002.

University Bookstore is open Monday through Friday. The cash sales for each week (Monday through Friday) are recorded on the following Monday as well as at the close of business on the last working day of each month.

The bookstore is primarily a cash and carry operation, but does provide charge sales to the faculty, staff, and departments of Fictitious University. Faculty and staff are allowed to charge with 3/10, n/45 terms. Charge sales are recorded and billed at the time of sale. A 7% sales tax is charged on all sales except sales to the departments of the University. The University is tax exempt.

Salaries are computed weekly (Monday through Friday) and paid the following Monday. Total salary for all employees is $430 per day during May. Ignore payroll deductions for this practice set.

The bookstore uses the perpetual inventory system.

All plant assets included in the May 24, 2002, Trial Balance were placed in service prior to June 1, 2001.

Transactions are recorded in a general journal and posted to a general ledger. Management does not feel the bookstore has enough charge customers nor vendors to warrant separate subsidiary ledgers for accounts receivable and accounts payable.

VERSION 1

JOURNAL ENTRIES FOR MAY 27 THROUGH MAY 31

May 27 $5,159 cash was received on cash sales for the week of May 20-24. The merchandise cost University Bookstore $4,127.

27 Collected a $3,000, 9%, 180-day note from Professor A. Griswold due today. Interest had not been accrued through Apr 30, 2002.

27 Sold $2,087 of merchandise on account to the athletic department. The merchandise sold cost $1,670.

27 Purchased for resale a complete line of greeting cards from S & W Nelson for $2,700. Terms 2/10, n/30.

27 Paid the salaries for May 20-24.

27 Sold 2,000 shares of $5 par value common stock for $18 per share.

28 Exchanged 500 shares of common stock for a used delivery van. The market value of the common stock is $19. The fair market value of the van is $10,000.

28 Received $750 in cash and a $1,750, 60-day, 12% note from Professor F. Fillwalk and granted a time extension on his past-due account. Professor Fillwalk is a major purchaser of statistical software.

28 Exchanged a display case placed in service on June 1, 1996, (original cost $7,500) for a new display case, list price $12,500, terms FOB destination. The trade-in allowance was $3,500 and the balance due was paid in cash. Freight costs are $65 and insurance in transit was $45. Display cases are classified as furniture.

29 Received full payment from Professor C. Humphrey for $750 of merchandise purchased from University Bookstore on May 20, 2002.

29 The athletic department returned $225 worth of merchandise. The cost of the merchandise was $180.

30 To implement an employee stock ownership plan, 1,600 shares of our own common stock were purchased on the open market at $20 per share.

30 800 shares of Treasury Stock-Common were distributed to employees as a bonus for a job well done. The bonus is considered to be salary and is expensed at cost.

30 To enlarge the selling space in the bookstore, bonds were issued and sold to cover the cost of remodeling. University Bookstore sold $100,000 par value, 5-year bonds, which pay semiannual interest of 12% on November 30 and May 30. The current market rate is 10%.

30 Returned $180 worth of damaged merchandise to S & W Nelson.

31 Declared the annual cash dividend of $22,350 to be allocated to Preferred and Common Stockholders. The dividend will be paid June 28, 2002, to stockholders of record on June 20, 2002. Dividends were last declared May 25, 2001.

31 The Board of Directors also declared a 5% common stock dividend to be issued June 28, 2002, to stockholders of record June 20. Market value today is $20.

31 Cash received on cash sales for the 5 days remaining in May totaled $6,654 (of which $435 is sales tax). The merchandise cost us $5,323.

31 Sold merchandise that cost us $2,900 on account to:

Business Department	$3,025
Professor C. Tomas	600 (plus tax)

31 Received notice that half of the remodeling is complete. The contractor submitted a bill for $50,000 which we paid today.

END OF FISCAL YEAR INFORMATION

Use May 31, 2002, (end of the fiscal year) as the transaction date for the adjusting entries.

A) The percentage of end-of-year bad debts is determined to be 5% of accounts receivable.

B) The marketable debt securities consist of 8% Treasury Bills purchased Jan 2, 2002, and paying interest every six months (July 2 and January 2).

C) An examination of the outstanding Notes Receivable revealed the following notes (assume no interest has been accrued):

J. Studyhard	$6,000, 11%,	6-month note dated 03/01/02
C. Mathwiz	$4,500, 11%,	1-year note dated 08/01/01
J. Weimers	$2,710, 9.5%,	9-month note dated 02/01/02
F. Fillwalk	$1,750, 11%,	60-day note dated 05/28/02

D) $1,832 of supplies are on hand at the end of the year.

NOTE: Remember to review your May 24, 2002, and May 31, 2002, Trial Balances to determine the additional adjusting entries.

VERSION 2

JOURNAL ENTRIES FOR MAY 27 THROUGH MAY 31

May 27 $4,927 cash was received on cash sales for the week of May 20-24 ($322 is sales tax). The merchandise cost University Bookstore $3,942.

27 Collected a $3,500, 8%, 120-day note from Professor A. Griswold due today. Interest had not been accrued through Apr 30, 2002.

27 Sold $1,850 of software on account to the business department. The merchandise sold cost $1,480.

27 Purchased for resale T-shirts with the school logo from S & W Nelson for $4,300. Terms 2/10, 1/15, n/30.

27 Paid the salaries for May 20-24.

28 Sold 2,000 shares of $5 par value common stock for $17 per share.

28 Exchanged 600 shares of common stock for a used delivery van. The market value of the common stock is $16. The fair market value of the van is $10,500.

28 Received $1,400 in cash and a $1,300, 90-day, 12% note from Professor F. Fillwalk and granted a time extension on his past-due account. Professor Fillwalk is a major purchaser of statistical software.

28 Exchanged a display case placed in service on June 1, 1996, (original cost $7,500) for a new display case, list price $12,750, terms FOB destination. The trade-in allowance was $1,950 and the balance due was paid in cash. Freight costs are $60 and insurance in transit was $55. Display cases are classified as furniture.

29 Received full payment from Professor C. Humphrey for $928 of merchandise purchased from University Bookstore on May 20, 2002.

29 The business department returned $167 worth of merchandise. The cost of the merchandise was $134.

30 To implement an employee stock ownership plan, 1,400 shares of our own common stock were purchased on the open market at $18 per share.

30 1,200 shares of Treasury Stock-Common were distributed to employees as a bonus for a job well done. The bonus is considered to be salary and is expensed at cost.

30 To enlarge the selling space in the bookstore, bonds were issued and sold to cover the cost of remodeling. University Bookstore sold $80,000 par value, 5-year bonds, which pay semiannual interest of 8% on November 30 and May 30. The current market rate is 10%.

30 Returned $375 worth of damaged merchandise to S & W Nelson.

31 Declared the annual cash dividend to Preferred and Common Stockholders to be paid June 28, 2002 to stockholders of record on June 20, 2002. A total of $24,600 will be paid out. Dividends were last declared May 25, 2001.

31 The Board of Directors also declared a 5% common stock dividend to be issued June 28, 2002, to stockholders of record June 20. Market value today is $18.

31 Cash received on cash sales for the 5 days remaining in May totaled $4,956. The merchandise cost us $3,965.

31 Sold merchandise that cost us $2,365 on account to:

Computer Science Department	$2,556
Professor C. Tomas	400 (plus tax)

31 Received notice that three-fourths of the remodeling is complete. The contractor submitted a bill for $60,000 which we paid today.

END OF FISCAL YEAR INFORMATION

Use May 31, 2002, (end of the fiscal year) as the transaction date for the adjusting entries.

A) The percentage of end-of-year bad debts is determined to be 6% of accounts receivable.

B) The marketable debt securities consist of 10% Treasury Bills purchased Jan 2, 2002, and paying interest every six months (July 2 and January 2).

C) An examination of the outstanding Notes Receivable revealed the following notes (assume no interest has been accrued):

J. Studyhard	\$4,500, 9%, 6-month note dated 03/01/02
C. Mathwiz	\$5,460, 9%, 1-year note dated 08/01/01
J. Weimers	\$2,750, 7.25%, 9-month note dated 02/01/02
F. Fillwalk	\$1,300, 12%, 90-day note dated 05/28/02

D) \$1,249 of supplies are on hand at the end of the year.

NOTE: Remember to review your May 24, 2002, and May 31, 2002, Trial Balances to determine the additional adjusting entries.

VERSION 3

JOURNAL ENTRIES FOR MAY 27 THROUGH MAY 31

May 27 $5,083 cash was received on cash sales for the week of May 20-24 ($332 is sales tax). The merchandise cost University Bookstore $3,801.

27 Collected $3,750 plus $94 interest from Professor A. Griswold for a note due today.

27 Sold $1,709 of stationery on account to the alumni office. The merchandise sold cost $1,367.

27 Purchased for resale T-shirts with the school logo from S & W Nelson for $6,800. Terms 2/10, 1/15, n/30.

27 Paid salaries for May 20-24.

27 Sold 3,500 shares of $5 par value common stock for $15 per share.

28 Exchanged 700 shares of common stock for a used delivery van. The market value of the common stock is $15. The fair market value of the van is $11,000.

28 Received $1,200 in cash and a $1,000, 90-day, 12% note from Professor F. Fillwalk and granted a time extension on his past-due account. Professor Fillwalk is a major purchaser of statistical software.

28 Exchanged a display case placed in service on June 1, 1996, (original cost $7,500) for a new display case, list price $11,000, terms FOB destination. The trade-in allowance was $3,000 and the balance due was paid in cash. Freight costs are $65 and insurance in transit was $35. Display cases are classified as furniture.

28 Received full payment from Professor C. Humphrey for $568 of merchandise purchased from University Bookstore on May 20, 2002.

29 The alumni office returned $432 worth of merchandise. The cost of the merchandise was $346.

30 To implement an employee stock ownership plan, 1,200 shares of our own common stock were purchased on the open market at $16 per share.

30 900 shares of Treasury Stock-Common were distributed to employees as a bonus for a job well done. This bonus is part of the employees' salary and is expensed at cost.

30 To enlarge the selling space in the bookstore, bonds were issued and sold to cover the cost of remodeling. University Bookstore sold $100,000 par value, 5-year bonds, which pay semiannual interest of 10% on November 30 and May 30. The current market rate is 8%.

30 Returned $352 worth of damaged merchandise to S & W Nelson.

31 Declared the annual cash dividend to Preferred and $.50 per share to Common Stockholders to be paid June 28, 2002 to stockholders of record June 20, 2002. Dividends were last declared May 25, 2001.

31 The Board of Directors also declared a 5% common stock dividend to be issued June 28, 2002, to stockholders of record June 20. Market value today is $15

31 Cash received on cash sales for the 5 days remaining in May totaled $4,657. The merchandise cost us $3,726.

31 Sold merchandise that cost us $1,732 on account to:

Computer Science Department	$1,410
Professor C. Thomas	755 (plus tax)

31 Payment of $75,000 for three-fourths of the remodeling is due today. The check was written and mailed.

END OF YEAR FISCAL INFORMATION

Use May 31, 2002, (end of the fiscal year) as the transaction date for the adjusting entries.

A) The percentage of end-of-year bad debts is determined to be 7% of accounts receivable.

B) The marketable debt securities consist of 10% Treasury Bills purchased Jan 2, 2002, and paying interest every six months (July 2 and Jan 2).

C) An examination of the outstanding Notes Receivable revealed the following notes (assume no interest has been accrued):

J. Studyhard	$4,400,	8.4%,	9-month note dated 03/01/02
C. Mathwiz	$5,000,	10%,	1-year note dated 08/01/01
J. Weimers	$2,760,	9.75%,	10-month note dated 11/01/01
F. Fillwalk	$1,300,	12%,	90-day note dated 05/28/02

D) $1,437 of supplies are on hand at the end of the year.

NOTE: Remember to review your May 24, 2002, and May 31, 2002, Trial Balances to determine the additional adjusting entries.

FINANCIAL ANALYSIS QUESTIONS - SET I

1. What do the following financial statements tell us?

   Income Statement
   Statement of Retained Earnings
   Balance Sheet

2. Compute the following liquidity ratios:

   a. current ratio

   b. acid-test ratio

   c. receivables turnover

   d. inventory turnover

3. Comment on the liquidity ratios.

4. Compute the following profitability ratios:

   a. profit margin

   b. asset turnover

   c. return on assets

   d. return on common stockholders equity

   e. earnings per share

   f. price-earnings ratio

   g. payout ratio

5. Comment on the profitability ratios.

FINANCIAL ANALYSIS QUESTIONS - SET II

1. Alice complained to Candie, "I'm a marketing major. I don't know why I can't just leave all these debits and credits to the accountants." Comment on this statement.

2. Going Broke Bank is processing a 5-year, $15,000 loan application for University Bookstore. The funds will be used to increase the inventory of the store. The company's liquidity must be evaluated to determine if the loan can be repaid. Compute the liquidity ratios and decide if the bank should grant the loan. Keep in mind that some of the cash the company has on hand may be committed for other purposes.

3. You have just won $30,000 in the state lottery. You must decide where to invest your money and are considering University Bookstore. Determine what ratios will help you make that decision and compute those ratios. Will you invest in this stock?

FINANCIAL ANALYSIS QUESTIONS - SET III

1. The dollar amounts on the financial statements do not tell the whole story. Comment on this statement.

2. State bank is processing a 5-year $10,000 loan application for University Bookstore. The company plans to use the money to purchase a new computer system. The company's financial position must be evaluated to determine if this loan will be granted.

   Would you grant the loan? Show the ratios to support your decision.

3. Your grandmother recently gave you a gift of $50,000. You are considering where to invest some or all of your money. Will University Bookstore be a consideration? Why or why not? Show supporting calculations.

4. As the accountant for University Bookstore, one of your duties is to present a financial report to the Board of Directors. Prepare a written report in good form following the instructions provided by your instructor.

University Bookstore, Inc.
Trial Balance
May 24, 2002

	Account Name	Trial Balance	
		Dr	Cr
101	Cash	19,685	
107	Marketable Debt Securities	42,000	
112	Accounts Receivable	5,930	
113	Allow for Doubtful Acc.		237
115	Notes Receivable	16,210	
118	Interest Receivable		
120	Merchandise Inventory	104,888	
126	Supplies	4,325	
130	Prepaid Insurance (3 year policy purchased 3/1/02)	18,000	
139	Construction in Process		
140	Land	151,000	
145	Building	500,000	
146	Accum. Depr-Buildings (Depreciated at 5% per year)		250,000
149	Furniture	74,790	
150	Accum. Depr-Furniture (Depreciated at 10% per year)		33,234
157	Equipment	16,050	
158	Accum. Depr-Equipment (Depreciated at 20% per year)		3,210
180	L T Marketable Securities (5% annual div received 2-1)	125,000	
201	Accounts Payable		23,250
212	Salaries Payable		
227	Sales Tax Payable		985
230	Interest Payable		
250	Pref Stk Dividends Pay		
251	Common Stock Div Pay		
268	Notes Payable (5-year, 9% note dated 2-1-02)		11,361
270	Bonds Payable		
273	Discount on Bonds Payable		
274	Premium on Bonds Payable		
275	Mortgage Payable (8.5% mortgage-interest paid on the 1st of each month)		273,630
311	Common Stock		200,000
312	PIC - Common Stock		32,000
313	Preferred Stock		60,000
315	PIC - Preferred Stock		
316	C.S. Dividend Distributable		
320	Retained Earnings		93,410
330	Treasury Stock-Common (1,000 shares using the cost method)	15,000	
331	PIC - Treasury Stock		
350	Income Summary		
401	Sales		984,320
412	Sales Returns & Allow	4,197	
414	Sales Discounts	1,171	
505	Cost of Goods Sold	708,985	
610	Advertising Expense	668	
612	Bad Debt Expense		
613	Credit Card Expense	13,504	
622	Repair Expense	4,328	
631	Supplies Expense		
635	Postage Expense	250	
636	Charitable Contributions Expense	5,000	
637	Service Charge Expense	300	

	Account Name	Trial Balance	
		Dr	Cr
711	Depreciation Expense		
722	Insurance Expense		
726	Salaries Expense	73,280	
730	Payroll Tax Expense	6,211	
732	Utilities Expense	33,392	
735	Miscellaneous Expense	785	
810	Dividend Revenue		10,000
820	Interest Revenue		1,500
826	Gain on Plant Assets		
905	Interest Expense	32,188	
921	Loss on Plant Assets		
	Totals	1,977,137	1,977,137

May 2002

SUNDAY	MONDAY	TUESDAY	WEDNESDAY	THURSDAY	FRIDAY	SATURDAY
			1	2	3	4
5	6	7	8	9	10	11
12	13	14	15	16	17	18
19	20	21	22	23	24	25
26	27	28	29	30	31	

THIS BALANCE SHEET IS TO BE USED TO COMPUTE THE RATIOS AND TO OBTAIN THE BEGINNING BALANCES FOR THE STATEMENT OF CASH FLOWS

University Bookstore, Inc.
Balance Sheet
June 1, 2001

ASSETS

CURRENT ASSETS			
Cash		25,149	
Marketable Debt Securities		42,000	
Accounts Receivable	4,625		
Allow. for Doubtful Acc	142	4,483	
Notes Receivable		8,000	
Interest Receivable		640	
Merchandise Inventory		69,773	
Supplies		1,543	
Prepaid Insurance		18,000	
Total Current Assets			169,588
PROPERTY PLANT & EQUIPMENT			
Land		151,000	
Building	500,000		
Acc Depr-Building	250,000	250,000	
Furniture	49,000		
Acc Depr-Furniture	33,234	15,766	
Equipment	13,530		
Acc Depr-Equipment	3,210	10,320	
Total Prop., Plant & Equipment			427,086
INVESTMENTS			
L T Marketable Securities			125,000
Total Assets			721,674

University Bookstore, Inc.
Balance Sheet
June 1, 2001

LIABILITIES & STOCKHOLDERS' EQUITY

CURRENT LIABILITIES		
Accounts Payable	15,900	
Salaries Payable	1,020	
Sales Tax Payable	904	
Interest Payable	1,907	
Pref Stk Dividends Pay	4,800	
Common Stk Div Pay	8,500	
Total Current Liabilities		33,031
LONG TERM LIABILITIES		
Notes Payable	11,000	
Mortgage Payable	307,233	
Total Long Term Liabilities		318,233
Total Liabilities		351,264
STOCKHOLDERS' EQUITY		
Common Stock	200,000	
PIC Common Stock	32,000	
Preferred Stock	60,000	
Retained Earnings	93,410	
	385,410	
Less: Treasury Stock	15,000	
Total Stockholders' Equity		370,410
Total Liabilities and Stockholders' Equity		721,674

TABLE B-1
PRESENT VALUE OF 1

(n) Periods	4%	5%	6%	8%	9%	10%	11%	12%	15%
1	.96154	.95238	.94340	.92593	.91743	.90909	.90090	.89286	.86957
2	.92456	.90703	.89000	.85734	.84168	.82645	.81162	.79719	.75614
3	.88900	.86384	.83962	.79383	.77218	.75132	.73119	.71178	.65752
4	.85480	.82270	.79209	.73503	.70843	.68301	.65873	.63552	.57175
5	.82193	.78353	.74726	.68058	.64993	.62092	.59345	.56743	.49718
6	.79031	.74622	.70496	.63017	.59627	.56447	.53464	.50663	.43233
7	.75992	.71068	.66506	.58349	.54703	.51316	.48166	.45235	.37594
8	.73069	.67684	.62741	.54027	.50187	.46651	.43393	.40388	.32690
9	.70259	.64461	.59190	.50025	.46043	.42410	.39092	.36061	.28426
10	.67556	.61391	.55839	.46319	.42241	.38554	.35218	.32197	.24719
11	.64958	.58468	.52679	.42888	.38753	.35049	.31728	.28748	.21494
12	.62460	.55684	.49697	.39711	.35554	.31863	.28584	.25668	.18691
13	.60057	.53032	.46884	.36770	.32618	.28966	.25751	.22917	.16253
14	.57748	.50507	.44230	.34046	.29925	.26333	.23199	.20462	.14133
15	.55526	.48102	.41727	.31524	.27454	.23939	.20900	.18270	.12289
16	.53391	.45811	.39365	.29189	.25187	.21763	.18829	.16312	.10687
17	.51337	.43630	.37136	.27027	.23107	.19785	.16963	.14564	.09293
18	.49363	.41552	.35034	.25025	.21199	.17986	.15282	.13004	.08081
19	.47464	.39573	.33051	.23171	.19449	.16351	.13768	.11611	.07027
20	.45639	.37689	.31180	.21455	.17843	.14864	.12403	.10367	.06110

TABLE B-1
PRESENT VALUE OF AN ANNUITY OF I

(n) Periods	4%	5%	6%	8%	9%	10%	11%	12%	15%
1	.96154	.95238	.94340	.92593	.91743	.90909	.90090	.89286	.86957
2	1.88609	1.85941	1.83339	1.78326	1.75911	1.73554	1.71252	1.69005	1.62571
3	2.77509	2.72325	2.67301	2.57710	2.53130	2.48685	2.44371	2.40183	2.28323
4	3.62990	3.54595	3.46511	3.31213	3.23972	3.16986	3.10245	3.03735	2.85498
5	4.45182	4.32948	4.21236	3.99271	3.88965	3.79079	3.69590	3.60478	3.35216
6	5.24214	5.07569	4.91732	4.62288	4.48592	4.35526	4.23054	4.11141	3.78448
7	6.00205	5.78637	5.58238	5.20637	5.03295	4.86842	4.71220	4.56376	4.16042
8	6.73274	6.46321	6.20979	5.74664	5.53482	5.33493	5.14612	4.96764	4.48732
9	7.43533	7.10782	6.80169	6.24689	5.99525	5.75902	5.53705	5.32825	4.77158
10	8.11090	7.72173	7.36009	6.71008	6.41766	6.14457	5.88923	5.65022	5.01877
11	8.76048	8.30641	7.88687	7.13896	6.80519	6.49506	6.20652	5.93770	5.23371
12	9.38507	8.86325	8.38384	7.53608	7.16073	6.81369	6.49236	6.19437	5.42062
13	9.98565	9.39357	8.85268	7.90378	7.48690	7.10336	6.74987	6.42355	5.58315
14	10.56312	9.89864	9.29498	8.24424	7.78615	7.36669	6.98187	6.62817	5.72448
15	11.11839	10.37966	9.71225	8.55948	8.06069	7.60608	7.19087	6.81086	5.84737
16	11.65230	10.83777	10.10590	8.85137	8.31256	7.82371	7.37916	6.97399	5.95424
17	12.16567	11.27407	10.47726	9.12164	8.54363	8.02155	7.54879	7.11963	6.04716
18	12.65930	11.68959	10.82760	9.37189	8.75563	8.20141	7.70162	7.24967	6.12797
19	13.13394	12.08532	11.15812	9.60360	8.95012	8.36492	7.83929	7.36578	6.19823
20	13.59033	12.46221	11.46992	9.81815	9.12855	8.51356	7.96333	7.46944	6.25933

General Journal

Date	Account Titles and Explanations	Ref.	Debit	Credit

General Journal

Date	Account Titles and Explanations	Ref.	Debit	Credit

General Journal

Date	Account Titles and Explanations	Ref.	Debit	Credit

General Journal

Date	Account Titles and Explanations	Ref.	Debit	Credit

General Journal

Date	Account Titles and Explanations	Ref.	Debit	Credit

Cash — No. 101

Date 2002	Explanation	Ref.	Debit	Credit	Balance
May 24	Balance				19685

Marketable Debt Securities — No. 107

Date 2002	Explanation	Ref.	Debit	Credit	Balance
May 24	Balance				42000

Accounts Receivable — No. 112

Date 2002	Explanation	Ref.	Debit	Credit	Balance
May 24	Balance				5930

Allowance for Doubtful Accounts — No. 113

Date 1998	Explanation	Ref.	Debit	Credit	Balance
July 24	Balance				237

Notes Receivable — No. 115

Date 1998	Explanation	Ref.	Debit	Credit	Balance
July 24	Balance				14210

Interest Receivable — No. 118

Date 1998	Explanation	Ref.	Debit	Credit	Balance

Merchandise Inventory — No. 120

Date 1998	Explanation	Ref.	Debit	Credit	Balance
July 24	Balance				104756

Supplies — No. 126

Date 2002	Explanation	Ref.	Debit	Credit	Balance
May 24	Balance				4325

Prepaid Insurance — No. 130

Date 2002	Explanation	Ref.	Debit	Credit	Balance
May 24	Balance				18000

Construction in Process — No. 139

Date 2002	Explanation	Ref.	Debit	Credit	Balance

Land — No. 140

Date 2002	Explanation	Ref.	Debit	Credit	Balance
May 24	Balance				151000

Buildings — No. 145

Date 2002	Explanation	Ref.	Debit	Credit	Balance
May 24	Balance				500000

Accum. Depr. Buildings — No. 146

Date 2002	Explanation	Ref.	Debit	Credit	Balance
May 24	Balance				250000

Furniture — No. 149

Date 2002	Explanation	Ref.	Debit	Credit	Balance
May 24	Balance				74790

Accum. Depr. Furniture — No. 150

Date 2002	Explanation	Ref.	Debit	Credit	Balance
May 24	Balance				33234

Equipment — No. 157

Date 2002	Explanation	Ref.	Debit	Credit	Balance
May 24	Balance				16050

Accum. Depr. Equipment — No. 158

Date 2002	Explanation	Ref.	Debit	Credit	Balance
May 24	Balance				3210

L. T. Marketable Equity Securities — No. 180

Date 2002	Explanation	Ref.	Debit	Credit	Balance
May 24	Balance				125000

Accounts Payable — No. 201

Date 2002	Explanation	Ref.	Debit	Credit	Balance
May 24	Balance				23250

Salaries Payable — No. 212

Date 2002	Explanation	Ref.	Debit	Credit	Balance

Sales Tax Payable — No. 227

Date 2002	Explanation	Ref.	Debit	Credit	Balance
May 24	Balance				985

Interest Payable — No. 230

Date 2002	Explanation	Ref.	Debit	Credit	Balance

Preferred Stock Dividends Payable — No. 250

Date 2002	Explanation	Ref.	Debit	Credit	Balance

Common Stock Dividends Payable — No. 251

Date 2002	Explanation	Ref.	Debit	Credit	Balance

Notes Payable — No. 268

Date 2002	Explanation	Ref.	Debit	Credit	Balance
May 24	Balance				11361

Bonds Payable — No. 270

Date 2002	Explanation	Ref.	Debit	Credit	Balance

Discount on Bonds Payable — No. 273

Date 2002	Explanation	Ref.	Debit	Credit	Balance

Premium on Bonds Payable — No. 274

Date 2002	Explanation	Ref.	Debit	Credit	Balance

Mortgage Payable — No. 275

Date 2002	Explanation	Ref.	Debit	Credit	Balance
May 24	Balance				273630

Common Stock — No. 311

Date 2002	Explanation	Ref.	Debit	Credit	Balance
May 24	Balance				200000

P-I-C in Excess of Par-Common — No. 312

Date 2002	Explanation	Ref.	Debit	Credit	Balance
May 24	Balance				32000

Preferred Stock — No. 313

Date 2002	Explanation	Ref.	Debit	Credit	Balance
May 24	Balance				60000

P-I-C in Excess of Par-Preferred — No. 315

Date 2002	Explanation	Ref.	Debit	Credit	Balance

Common Stock Div Distributable — No. 316

Date 2002	Explanation	Ref.	Debit	Credit	Balance

Retained Earnings — No. 320

Date 2002	Explanation	Ref.	Debit	Credit	Balance
May 24	Balance				93410

Treasury Stock-Common No. 330

Date 2002	Explanation	Ref.	Debit	Credit	Balance
May 24	Balance				15000

P-I-C - Treasury Stock No. 331

Date 2002	Explanation	Ref.	Debit	Credit	Balance

Income Summary No. 350

Date 2002	Explanation	Ref.	Debit	Credit	Balance

Sales No. 401

Date 2002	Explanation	Ref.	Debit	Credit	Balance
May 24	Balance				984320

Sales Returns and Allowances — No. 412

Date 2002	Explanation	Ref.	Debit	Credit	Balance
May 24	Balance				4197

Sales Discounts — No. 414

Date 2002	Explanation	Ref.	Debit	Credit	Balance
May 24	Balance				1171

Cost of Goods Sold — No. 505

Date 2002	Explanation	Ref.	Debit	Credit	Balance
May 24	Balance				708985

Advertising Expense — No. 610

Date 2002	Explanation	Ref.	Debit	Credit	Balance
May 24	Balance				668

Bad Debts Expense — No. 612

Date 2002	Explanation	Ref.	Debit	Credit	Balance

Credit Card Expense — No. 613

Date 2002	Explanation	Ref.	Debit	Credit	Balance
May 24	Balance				13504

Repair Expense — No. 622

Date 2002	Explanation	Ref.	Debit	Credit	Balance
May 24	Balance				4328

Supplies Expense — No. 631

Date 2002	Explanation	Ref.	Debit	Credit	Balance

Postage Expense — No. 635

Date 2002	Explanation	Ref.	Debit	Credit	Balance
May 24	Balance				250

Charitable Contributions Expense — No. 636

Date 2002	Explanation	Ref.	Debit	Credit	Balance
May 24	Balance				5000

Service Charge Expense — No. 637

Date 2002	Explanation	Ref.	Debit	Credit	Balance
May 24	Balance				300

Depreciation Expense — No. 711

Date 2002	Explanation	Ref.	Debit	Credit	Balance

Insurance Expense — No. 722

Date 2002	Explanation	Ref.	Debit	Credit	Balance

Salaries Expense — No. 726

Date 2002	Explanation	Ref.	Debit	Credit	Balance
May 24	Balance				73280

Payroll Tax Expense — No. 730

Date 2002	Explanation	Ref.	Debit	Credit	Balance
May 24	Balance				6211

Utilities Expense — No. 732

Date 2002	Explanation	Ref.	Debit	Credit	Balance
May 24	Balance				33392

Miscellaneous Expense — No. 735

Date 2002	Explanation	Ref.	Debit	Credit	Balance
May 24	Balance				785

Dividend Revenue — No. 810

Date 2002	Explanation	Ref.	Debit	Credit	Balance
May 24	Balance				10000

Interest Revenue — No. 820

Date 2002	Explanation	Ref.	Debit	Credit	Balance
May 24	Balance				1500

Gain on Plant Assets — No. 826

Date 2002	Explanation	Ref.	Debit	Credit	Balance

Interest Expense — No. 905

Date 2002	Explanation	Ref.	Debit	Credit	Balance
May 24	Balance				32188

Loss on Plant Assets — No. 921

Date 2002	Explanation	Ref.	Debit	Credit	Balance

ACCOUNT TITLES	TRIAL BALANCE DR.	TRIAL BALANCE CR.	ADJUSTMENTS DR.	ADJUSTMENTS CR.
Cash				
Marketable Debt Securities				
Accounts Receivable				
Allow. for Doubtful Accounts				
Notes Receivable				
Interest Receivable				
Merchandise Inventory				
Supplies				
Prepaid Insurance				
Construction in Process				
Land				
Buildings				
Accum. Depr. - Buildings				
Furniture				
Accum. Depr. - Furniture				
Equipment				
Accum. Depr. - Equipment				
L.T. Marketable Equity Securities				
Accounts Payable				
Salaries Payable				
Sales Tax Payable				
Interest Payable				
Preferred Stk Dividends Payable				
Common Stk Dividends Payable				
Notes Payable				
Bonds Payable				
Discount Bonds Payable				
Premium Bonds Payable				
Mortgage Payable				
Common Stock				
PIC - Common Stock				
Preferred Stock				
PIC - Pfd. Stock				
C. S. Div Distributable				
Retained Earnings				
Treasury Stock				
PIC - Treasury Stock				
Sales				
Sales Returns & Allow.				
Sales Discounts				
Cost of Goods Sold				
Advertising Expense				
Bad Debts Expense				
Credit Card Expense				
Repair Expense				
Supplies Expense				
Postage Expense				
Charitable Contributions Expense				

ADJUSTED TRIAL BALANCE		INCOME STATEMENT		BALANCE SHEET	
DR.	CR.	DR.	CR.	DR.	CR.

	TRIAL BALANCE		ADJUSTMENTS	
ACCOUNT TITLES	DR.	CR.	DR.	CR.
Service Charge Expense				
Depreciation Expense				
Insurance Expense				
Salaries Expense				
Payroll Tax Expense				
Utilities Expense				
Miscellaneous Expense				
Dividend Revenue				
Interest Revenue				
Gain on Plant Assets				
Interest Expense				
Loss on Plant Assets				
Total				

ADJUSTED TRIAL BALANCE		INCOME STATEMENT		BALANCE SHEET	
DR.	CR.	DR.	CR.	DR.	CR.

UNIVERSITY BOOKSTORE, INC.
Income Statement
For the Year Ended May 31, 2002

UNIVERSITY BOOKSTORE, INC.
Statement of Retained Earnings
For the Year Ended May 31, 2002

UNIVERSITY BOOKSTORE, INC.
Balance Sheet
May 31, 2002

Assets

(Continued)

UNIVERSITY BOOKSTORE, INC.
Balance Sheet
May 31, 2002

Liabilities and Owner's Equity

UNIVERSITY BOOKSTORE, INC.
Post-Closing Trial Balance
May 31, 2002

	Debit	Credit

UNIVERSITY BOOKSTORE, INC.
Statement of Cash Flows
For the Year Ended May 31, 2002